HOW DOES IT GROW?

FOX

by Jinny Johnson
Illustrations by Graham Rosewarne

A⁺
Smart Apple Media

Smart Apple Media
P.O. Box 3263, Mankato, MN 56002

Printed in the United States of America

Library of Congress Cataloging-in-Publication Data

Johnson, Jinny.
  Fox / Jinny Johnson ; illustrations by Graham Rosewarne.
    p. cm. -- (How does it grow?)
  Includes index.
  ISBN 978-1-59920-354-6 (hardcover)
  1. Foxes--Life cycles--Juvenile literature. I. Rosewarne, Graham, ill. II. Title.
  QL737.C22J644 2010
  599.775'156--dc22

                                                  2008053340

All words in **bold** can be found in the glossary on page 30.

Designed by Helen James
Edited by Mary-Jane Wilkins
Picture research by Su Alexander

Photograph acknowledgements
page 9 Phyllis Greenberg/Photolibrary Group;
13 AlaskaStock/Photolibrary Group; 23 Photolibrary Group;
29 Elliott Neep/Photolibrary Group
Front cover Elliott Neep/Photolibrary Group

9 8 7 6 5 4 3 2 1

Contents

First Days

These baby red foxes were born just a few days ago. They lie snuggled up to their mother in their **den**. The den is a hole dug in the ground. It may be near a hedge, by a tree, or even under a garden shed.

A baby fox is tiny, and he cannot see or hear. He's not much longer than your hand, and he weighs less than an apple. His soft dark fur keeps him warm.

Baby foxes are called **cubs** or kits. All they can do at a few days old is sleep and eat.

MOM KEEPS THE BABY FOXES SAFE AND WARM.

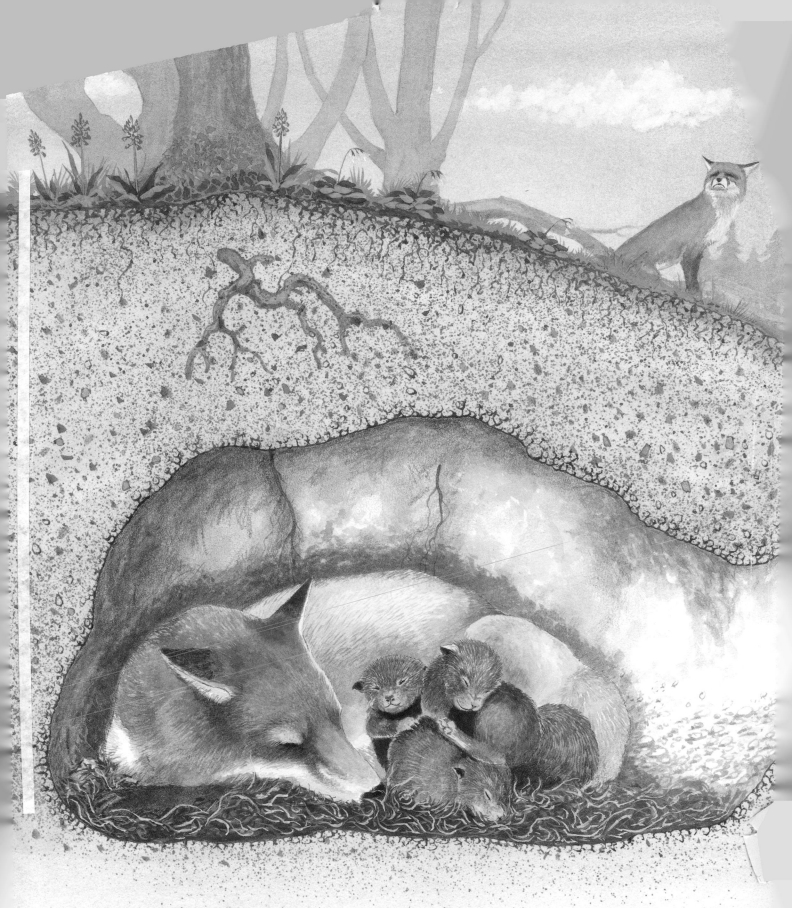

The baby foxes are hungry. What do they eat?

Inside the Den

Mom's milk is all the cubs need
for the first few weeks of their lives.
Her milk is rich and the cubs grow fast.

The mother fox doesn't leave her family.
Her **mate** brings food to her in the den so
she doesn't need to go **hunting**.

When a fox cub is about two weeks
old, his eyes begin to open. He starts
to explore the den with his brothers
and sisters, but they are not big enough
to go outside yet.

THE MALE FOX BRINGS
FOOD TO HIS MATE.

The baby foxes are growing bigger.
When will they go outside?

What's Outside?

When he is about four weeks old, the fox cub peeks out of the den for the first time. He and his brothers and sisters don't dare go far from home.

If the cubs get scared, they call to their mom and she comes running to the rescue. Mom gently picks up the cubs by the skin at the back of their neck and carries them back to the den.

Soon the cub's baby fur falls out and he grows a new reddish coat. He begins to look more like his mom and dad.

THE WORLD OUTSIDE THE
DEN LOOKS SCARY AT FIRST.

*What do the fox cubs
do when they go outside?*

Playtime

The cubs have lots of fun when they're outside. They are very curious about the world. They sniff around and chew on anything they find.

The cubs like to chase each other and pounce. They love to play, but they are also practicing for when they are full grown. Then they will hunt and catch other animals to eat.

What do the cubs eat now?

What's for Supper?

The growing cubs are very hungry and need more food. Their mother and father bring them mice, and other small animals.

When mom and dad arrive with a meal, they call to the cubs. The cubs rush up as fast as they can, yelping and wagging their tails. They can't wait for their food and may fight over it.

The parents start to leave food further away from the den to encourage the cubs to explore.

THE CUBS CAN'T
CATCH THEIR OWN
FOOD YET.

When will the cubs start to learn to hunt?

Lots to Learn

At three months, the cubs are big enough to follow their parents when they go hunting for food. At first the cubs watch and learn. They have to find out what is good to eat.

When the family is out, mom keeps a close eye on the cubs. If she's worried, she uses a special bark. The cubs know this means danger.

The cubs look more like their parents now. Their ears are bigger and their faces are longer and narrower.

THE MOTHER FOX WATCHES THE CUBS WHEN THEY ARE OUT OF THE DEN.

What do the cubs try to catch?

Hunting Practice

The first creatures the cubs learn to catch are worms and beetles. They listen carefully to hear them moving along the ground and then pounce.

As the cubs practice and grow, they will start catching mice, rabbits, and other animals to eat.

Like their parents, the cubs gobble up lots of berries and other fruits. They pick up food left by humans, too.

CATCHING SMALL CREATURES SUCH AS WORMS IS GOOD HUNTING PRACTICE.

When will the cubs be full grown?

Time to Leave

At six months, the cubs are almost
as big as their mom and weigh
a bit more than a pet cat. They will
soon be able to live on their own.

The parents bring less food now.
The cubs have to hunt for themselves
most of the time, and it's not always easy.

The cubs can run fast to escape from
danger. They also chase fast **prey** animals.
They have lots of sharp teeth for eating
their prey.

YOUNG FOXES MUST
LEARN HOW TO WATCH
AND SNEAK UP ON PREY.

Are the cubs ready to leave home?

Finding a Home

In autumn, the cubs leave. There is not enough food for them all nearby, so the young foxes go elsewhere to live.

If a young male wanders into an area where another fox is living, he will be attacked and driven away. When he finds a safe place, he **marks** the trees, fences, or walls with his own **scent** so other animals know that he is there.

A female cub may stay with her parents longer. If there is lots of food, she may help mom raise her cubs next spring.

A FOX MARKS ITS HOME RANGE WITH ITS URINE.

What does the young fox do all by himself?

Living Alone

When the young fox has found
a place to live, he spends a lot of time
finding food. He's always on the
lookout for a meal.

His hearing is so good that he can
hear a mouse scurrying through the
grass. The fox is ready to pounce.
His sense of smell is very keen too.

When the fox finds lots of food,
he may hide some to eat another time.
He buries it or covers it with leaves
and hopes another fox won't find it!

FOXES CAN RUN FAST
ENOUGH TO CATCH
SQUIRRELS TO EAT.

What do foxes do in the winter?

Starting a Family

Life is harder in winter. The weather is cold and food is hard to find.

Luckily the fox has thick fur to keep him warm. When he settles down to sleep, he wraps his big bushy tail around himself like a cozy scarf.

The fox has been alone since he left his family. Early in the new year, he notices a young **vixen** nearby. It is time to start their own family.

How do the foxes get ready for their cubs?

New Life

The foxes search for a den. It must be big enough for the vixen and her cubs to live in for the first few weeks. The den needs to be near fresh water, but well hidden so they are safe.

The foxes mate. After about seven weeks, the vixen gives birth in the den and soon her tiny cubs are feeding on her milk.

The baby foxes are small now, but this time next year, they may be having cubs of their own.

THE FOXES NEED A SAFE DEN WHERE THEY CAN BRING UP THEIR FAMILY.

More About Foxes

What animal family do foxes belong to?

A fox is a **mammal**. It belongs to the dog family and is related to dogs, wolves, and coyotes. There are many different types of foxes. Some of the best known are the Arctic fox, which lives in the far north, and the tiny fennec fox found in desert areas of North Africa. The red fox is also common.

Where does the red fox live?

The red fox is one of the most widespread of all mammals. It lives all over North America, Europe, North Africa, and much of Asia. Red foxes were taken to Australia in the 19th century and are now common there. Foxes are very adaptable creatures.

How big is a fox?

A red fox weighs 9 to 18 pounds (4 to 8 kg). Its head and body are 24 to 28 inches (62 to 72 cm) long. The bushy tail can be up to 17 inches (44 cm) long. Female foxes are slightly smaller than males.

THE RED FOX IS A CLEVER ANIMAL AND A FAST-MOVING HUNTER.

Words to Remember

cub
A young mammal, such as a fox or bear

den
A fox's home, often a hole dug in the ground

hunting
Finding and catching other animals to eat

mammal
A warm-blooded animal, usually with some hair on its body. Female mammals feed milk to their young.

mark
When an animal puts its own scent on an object. It's a way of saying, "I live here."

mate
Male and female animals pair up, or mate, to produce young. An animal's partner is its mate.

prey
An animal that is hunted and eaten by another animal.

scent
The smell of urine used used by an animal to mark where it lives.

vixen
A female fox.

Web Sites

For Students
National Geographic
http://animals.nationalgeographic.com/animals/mammals/
red-fox.html

Life Cycle, Characteristics, and Behaviors of the Red Fox
http://www.nhptv.org/NatureWorks/redfox.html

North American Mammals
http://www.mnh.si.edu/mna/about.cfm

For Teachers
Lesson Plan and Simple Activity on Foxes
http://atozteacherstuff.com/pages/480.shtml

Animal Life Cycles Lessons
http://www.col-ed.org/cur/sci/sci15.txt

Index